AF601785

INTRODUCTION

Words can carry us to places within an instant, a whole world appears within our imagination without any conscious effort. A wordsmith crafts words upon the lathe of the psyche to fashion them and arrange them. From the initial spark of inspiration is borne a new realm of adventure within our mind's.

Presented within these pages you will find a selection of poems that focus upon our spiritual connection to all in nature, indeed we are nature. A poetic mind has many a muse but my muse of muses is the Earth herself.

*** the cover photograph is an actual photograph of a face i saw in an Ash tree by a healing well near Broughton, Northamptonshire, U.K - 2007.**

THE EARTH IS DREAMING

the Earth is dreaming to the Moon`s lullaby
the Earth is dreaming with a tearful eye
the Earth is dreaming to awaken visions
the Earth is dreaming and making decisions

The Earth is dreaming of different ways
the Earth is dreaming within all our days
the Earth is dreaming of things that are strange
the Earth is dreaming of all we arrange

The Earth is dreaming of plentiful grain
the Earth is dreaming to protect her name
the Earth is dreaming and seeing what grows
the Earth is dreaming accounting with crows

The Earth is dreaming and dreaming awake
the Earth is dreaming of mountains that shake
the Earth is dreaming of wasteful toil
the Earth is dreaming of replenished fertile soil

The Earth is dreaming though turns not to sleep
the Earth is dreaming but to us she speaks

Knap Hill Neolithic Causewayed Enclosure, Northeast of Alton Barnes, Wiltshire, U.K.

View from the parking area near the summit, as the Moon was rising through the Hawthorn tree. Just below the summit you can see the ditchres of the causewayed enclosure.

Photography by the author - 2007

THE LANGUAGE OF NATURE

What words are whispered amidst green leaves
high up on their branches catching light for the trees
what wisdom is spoken by the flower and the bee
what song is there sung in their sacred harmony

What is there spoken in the lay of the land
what words lie unbroken in what tongue to understand
what can be heard by the wild water's side
in voices so many over stones passing by

What message does a call from a bird bring swift
from the heart of nature and hard to be missed
what echo returns that calls to the soul
in the language of nature that speaks to us all.

Swallowhead Springs, the source of the River Kennet, near West Kennet Long Barrow and Silbury Hill, Wiltshire, U.K.

Sawllowhead Springs is an ancient sacred place of palpable energy.

Incidentally, the bridge where the river Kennet flows past Silbury Hill and under the A4 (old Roman road) is called Pan bridge. Pan is the Greek god of the wild, shepherds and flocks, mountainous wilds, rustic music and companion of the Nymphs, he has the hindquarters, legs and horns of a goat. Nymphs are divine spirits who animate nature and love to dance and sing and dwell within mountainous places, forests and by lakes and streams.

Photography by the author - 2007.

LISTEN TO THE EARTH

There was once a time that we may return again
in half forgotten fables that tell of the story when
many mighty stones were there across the sacred land
still they whisper to those that care that listen if they can

For so far that we`ve come we`ve lost our sight of Earth
so far away from the rites that held our place of birth
of the green man and the corn, the Goddess in the land
lets listen to the Earth again, so come now take my hand

I`ll lead you to the faerie fey for they reside at will
in a place not on this Earth but found within the hills
they too like the old ones see the passing years
that lead on to eternity, within their timeless spheres

What then shall befall us if we disconnect ourselves
from enchanted faerie glens and no more speak of elves?
all the magic that binds us to the very Earth around
for answers lie within herself, within her sacred ground

No matter how we perceive the truth shall always hold
from the wisdom of the old ones to the faerie kin extolled
if we foster compassion each within our hearts

we can hear the beat of Earth, the rhythm of the dance

unfolding for eternity in deep felt mirth, entranced

View from within a crop formation in a field of Barley of Silbury Hill, a Neolithic chalk and earth stepped spiral mound, Wiltshire, U.K.

Photography by the author - 2010

DRAGON OF THE EARTH

The dragon that lies within the land

known throughout time

and under the lines of the ley

as Earth energy that comes to rise

and spiral where it may

a potent force that gathers from the deep

to rise up through the earth

and once I believe harnessed

and set to work

where by the stones that mark it`s course

channel and focus this serpent like horse

though by agreement of mutual worth

measured by respect

for the dragon of the Earth

Were then, some of the white horses that we see

from Uffington Hill

to Wiltshire`s chalky Avalonian vales

once in the form of dragons with tails?

so named is such a mound

to be found close by to the giant white beast

who`s sheer size astounds

those who climb upon it`s back

Dragon Hill to be exact

close by to the ancient Ridgeway track

Did they tell of the tales that told

of the dragon lines

that wind. never straight but serpentine

of lore forgotten but still there to find?

And let us not forget Silbury Hill

having stood 5,000 years and more and standing still

as a testament to those times

when much was known of those dragon lines

this sacred spiral serpent mound

where the dragon rose and rises still

up to the sky bejewelled by stars

and back down again to the ground

Within the Earth the dragon dreams

sleeping sometimes but sure to awake

and sometimes even "seen" by those who can

if they possess the second sight

shimmering with electric light

as the dragon of the Earth

that winds through time

and comes to coil within our minds

Pine tree rings, Bucknell wood, near Towcester, Northamptonshire, U.K.

Photography by the author - 2007

THE WILDWOOD WITHIN

The morning mist now gently kissed

by the rising disc of the Sun

nostrils flare and sniff the fresh dampened air

listening now

the horned one surveys all that surrounds

before returning once again

to the woodland of his grounds

The owl calls from distant there within
as the blackbirds begin to sing
as the morning grows in glory
as the dawn slips away.
In the meadow by the brook
wild eyed hares leap and play

Enchanted by the wildwood`s call
touched by the very sanctity of life
called to a wild place within
to far forgotten days
when robin in the hood the spirit of the wood
and those that dwelled amidst the green
were more closely understood

As the pipes of Pan begin to play
the horned one some call Herne
and some call cernunnos
with great vigour leads the way
to the primeval part of us that knows
the very essence of nature
that shall ever flow
within our hearts
within our blood
and within our bones
to the balance of all things
that the Goddess has ordained

as sacred in her name

*** Robin is an old English word for spirit**
Hood is an old English word for wood.

The healing energy of trees can not only be felt but sometimes can also be seen.

A stand of trees, near the source of the The *Sèvre* Niortaise river near **Sepvret in Western France** in the Deux-*Sèvres* département, that flows into the Atlantic Ocean.

Photography by the author - 2010

A MOMENT OUT OF TIME

How the world seems kinder
when your thoughts all fall at ease
When feeling bright our hearts delight
upon such gentle breeze

Much there is that we can find
sublime and full of charm
this healing space that sees no haste
where there can be no harm

But for a moment out of time
serene and somewhere free
receiving this, a granted wish
no time brings more to please.

That which has now come to thee
resonates so fine
recalling dreams, forgotten themes
the world has left behind

Seize the day that brings thee bliss

how can we do much more

and all that is, that was that is

returns again for sure

Knowing that whatever comes

can`t steal this from our minds

upon the day we stole away

in a moment out of time

Barley softly sways and sings a sweeping song as it rustles with the breeze.

a field of barley next to Silbury Hill, Wiltshire, U.K.

photgraphy by the author - 2010

ENOSHA`S DREAM

As i lay in reverie

upon Wayland Smithy's mound

half awaking from a dream

on such a sacred ground

i heard a lady say to me

as clearly as the day

just two simple whispered words

that somehow seemed profound

"Enosha's dream" i heard her say

then no more then did she speak

but so refreshed was i that day

by my reverie

i rose up from that place

from my sanctuary of sleep

upon Wayland`s mound

where i was cradled deep

In this place of ancient rites
hallowed pagan shrine
did you here then preside
by an altar to divine?
or did you come to this place
that many still hold dear
an acolyte to worship
what the powers came to fear?

Long before the church did smite
with such a heavy hand
that breached into the pagan heart
and reached across the land
long before those wretched days
of outlawed pagan ways
our ancestors to the Earth
Goddess homage made

Wayland Smithy, near the Ridgeway Track, Oxfordshire, U.K.

Photography by the author - 2010

WITHIN HER HANDS

For one to hold within their hands

a precious gem so very rare

knowing it`s worth beyond all compare

would not they wish that it not drop

lie broken by lack of care?

The Earth is such a many faceted jewel

sharing and caring, though sometimes destroying

in all her greatness great and small

Now once we had an understanding

a way of more harmoniously existing

making careful use of each resource

but what began with simple needs

gathering, hunting, planting seeds

with the need to harvest fare

became the rape of land and air

The waters from her sacred springs

tainted some, by death machines

but like the river flowing on

we can become to see as one

She beckons us within her ways

calling clarion that we may

breathe as one upon this land

and see the precious gem in hand

for she holds us in her care

and with her then we need to share

not just take to make all

the fattest bellies remain full

as the more we take in our abstraction

fatal becomes this world`s attraction

and as all the children need to know

all things come but sometimes go

Walker's Hill (with Adam's Grave - burial mound on top) to the left of the photograph and Knap Hill to the right define the Goddess in the land lying down on her side with the top half of her body twisted to the sky. Knap Hill becomes her left thigh whilst adam's grave atop walker's hill becomes her right breast, as viewed from East Field, Alton Barnes, Wiltshire, U.K.

Photography by the author - 2010

WITHIN THE GREENWOOD GLADE

Come enter the greenwood
answer Bealtaine's call
leave aside past season's woes
for now no leaves do fall
if only for a spell they go
then cast your mind to play
for new loves with hearts aglow
are greening in the May

To bind their dreams as they entwine
within the glade unseen
with the joy of columbine
the ivy grows so keen
the scent of blooms pervades the air
come drink a hearty fill
for nature nurtures all with care
the glory of her will

In the grass so verdant green
lies the morning dew

the spider's web no more unseen

beaded now to view

reveals within it`s tapestry

the subtle flow of life

for weaved within the chemistry

more than meets the eye

*** Bealtaine: Gaelic May festival - pronounced B`yul-tin-ar**

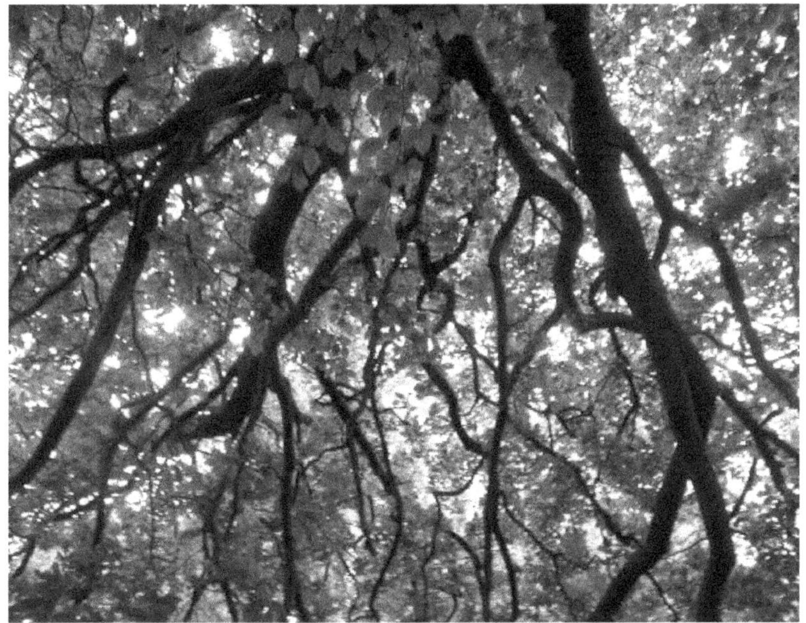

Beech Tree Canopy, Avebury Stone Circle, Wiltshire, U.K

Photography by the author - 2010

THE SISTERS OF WYRD

Like a sailor who sails the seven seas

seeking as they sail for their golden ship of dreams

set sail on some destiny

where fate and fortune change the wyrd web we see

All those things that we thought we had planned
oh for the lines that lie upon our hands
and the rainbow is only ever true
right where you stand and not some other's view

Like a moth too close to the flame
lured by something bright that may lead us blind
to where we wish we had never came
given wings to fly as the wyrd web unwinds

Such a thing the wyrd sisters weave
by our actions we may learn by all that we perceive
taking account of ourselves
with each silver strand into the web we delve

As we go we can change our path
for many strands may lead to the things that we may need
and all that we see is what we are
in all this universe in each and every star

Upon our travels that may take us far
sometimes the hurt that we feel leaves with us a scar
All this the wyrd sisters weave
all things that through many ways we come to perceive

As the wyrd sisters weave along your trail

consider the cup that you hold may not be full of jewels

but all that is revealed becomes our quested grail

A WYRD WORLD AND THE GODDESSES OF DESTINY

WYRD

Wyrd is the life we live and that which shall become. Wyrd is a web upon which we navigate our paths where each step creates a vibration that ripples out across all the strands of the wyrd web of life. Wyrd is life interconnecting, nothing exists entire of itself, it is cause and effect, balance and responsibility.

THE THREE NORNS

In Saxon mythology Wyrd carries the same meaning portrayed in Nordic mythology by The Three Norns (there is a thin line between Nordic and Saxon mythology and ancient art) The Three Norns are the Goddesses of destiny and they are called Urd "What Once Was" Verdandi "What Is Coming into Being" and Skuld "What Shall Be". The Wyrd Sisters in Shakespear's play A Midsummer's Night Dream were based upon the three norns.

Glastonbury Tor and St Michael's Tower, all that remains of the 14th century church that once stood atop the tor.

It is also known as the Isle of Avalon. Two thousand years ago the sea washed up to the foot of the Tor, so it would have been an island. Avalon was also called the isle of glass and it would have appeared that it was on glass when surrounded by water. Ancient myth tells of Avalon as being the meeting place of the dead, a liminal realm where the sea meets the land and there is a legend that king Arthur was buried upon the Isle of Avalon. Welsh tradition sees the Tor as the home of Gywn Ap Nudd, lord of the underworld, a place where fairies live.

Around the Tor and winding up to the top is a system of terraces that some suggest are man made, they are weathered but still well definded so if you fancy another way to the summit then walking the terraces is an interesting option.

Legend has it that Joseph of Arimathea (jesus's uncle) buried the grail cup from jesus's last supper at the foot of the Tor.

At the base of the Tor is Chalice well, the water has a reddish tinge to it due to it's iron rich content.

Photography by the author - 2010

ALL SOULS KNOW WELL OF SOULS

The tangled path of time obscure

yet with wit we can traverse

all the woes that we endure

to reach the well with mighty thirst

Shining each in radiant light

unfettered our wings, unfurled ascend

to the well of souls we take our flight

where ancient hearts may meet again

The source of us, become immersed

drink deeply of the waters there

where gathered souls have come to share

where wisdom sings within the air

Back to the Earth we may choose to go

to see again through worldly eyes

yet that choice is hard to tell

upon returning from the well

ANOTHER SPIRIT LEVEL:

THE SPIRIT OF H20

(a reflection upon and within water)

What a clear thought can achieve

by the solution of water

that flows with ease

is anything that we please

homoeopathically distilling

whatever is given

the wonder of water

is a blessing indeed

Water it seems has many solutions

by whatever it holds

within it`s dimension

the water that we bless

is water at it`s best

and wherever in this world

you may be

water reaches thee
flowing into the streams
into the rivers
and into the sea
can we then see a world in love
unconditional, joyful and free?

So let`s drink a toast
to the mighty water spirit
molecular, dynamic
crystalline and clear
raising consciousness on our planet
by the magic of water
may our visions appear

Any intention exerted
whether large or small
can create a change
from a giant wave tsunami
to a wonderful waterfall

If you speak to water
it reacts within its system
corresponding to your intent
then taking shape to implement

within its structure, cellular change

and once within the system

flows where water flows

into the streams into the rivers

into the oceans of the world

carrying the words that you gave it

that shape its inner form

the water then to be drunk

imbued by one and all

then what was given

as we are water based

becomes the way that we feel

and the way that we relate

So lets give love to water

by the power of our words

and stop and think!

each time we drink

about how we wish to be

maybe this world we can refresh

by water's wonderful memory?

FLUTTER BY WINGS

With wings that flutter myriad

in utter splendid colour

but butter not are they

as they grace the garden

that attracts them to its elegant array

of Lepidoptera enticing flora

and once discovered

shall return each day

within their short span of life

or so it seems to us

who watch them flutter by

though it is fair to say

that they have two lives within one

and somewhere in the middle

get reformed and then reborn

from the caterpillar within the cocoon

the chrysalis that someday soon

shall yield the insect from within

completely changed from it`s former self

now adorned with splendid wings
to greet the day anen

THE CELTIC FLUTTER BY SOUL

Going back to times of yore

long, long before these days

where in the meadows

the flutter bys flexed their wings

and without the reflex of pins

alighted upon the wild flowers

free and without a care

so splendid as they are

they inspired the Celtic bards

to consider yet again who we really are

our own span of life and beyond to stars

this they did and they came to see

that the flutter-by was a soul

that had flown to the summer land

and now returned with wings so grand

and so what they knew too to be a flutter-by

and then so aptly termed

were the ancestors and the ones they loved

here again from the sweet fields above

and not something to be stuck with pins

but respected and cared for

these flutter-by wings

as those that return again and are reborn

not just in metaphor but also in form

manifested anew to greet a new dawn

Swallowtail butterfly, Loubigne, western France.

Photography by the author - 2010

BEHOLD THE BEE

Behold the humble honey bee

as it stumbles into flowers

pollinating as it goes

buzzing and brimming

with life giving powers

gathering sweet nectar

to honey your mead

and wax for the candles

that at night we may need

The humble honey bee

who shares it`s industry freely

to sweeten your bread

who by it`s labour may nurse a cold

with this food of the Gods

from days of old

known for it`s powers

to preserve and protect

for vitality and much more yet!

So set your thoughts to such a thing as a bee

as to be a bee that daily dives

from flower to flower

and back again to the hive

is to be free and to be free is to be alive

So blessed be the humble honey bee!

but where would we be if it was gone?

this one that is solar driven in it`s song

through all the days that seem so long

in sweet summers alchemy

where would we be?

Some things you see cannot be replaced

save for maybe our own human race

as we alone cannot go on

depending as we do upon

such things as the one who is solar driven in it`s song

through all the days that seem so long

in sweet summer's alchemy

So then it seems to be

that we cannot be without the BEE

Bumble Bee taking nectar from Lavender, Lounigne, Western France.

Photography by the author - 2010

ONE in LOVE

Each distant star carries with it a memory of our soul
our hearts are synchronised with the music of the spheres
our bodies are crystallised components of the Gods

Contained within each of us is the eternal chord
struck once at the very emergence of our universe

it holds our form, that which we choose to be, that which we dream we are

is not all life therefore magic, a shimmering facet of our desires?

Climbing the inner temple of our bodies

we reach the centre from which we observe all things

we open ourselves to realities that know no bounds or separation

only unity in divinity, that which we are

Casting aside the mask of illusion we see with eyes of awareness

perceiving our nature as a force of great power

free flowing thoughts that carry the whisper of bliss

bring joy to our lips as we acknowledge this

for our true strength lies within a smile that generates love and kindness

Compassion is the seed that flowers into love

that brings us back to us and links us into a hive of harmony

our consciousness unified

Is it not better to be ONE in LOVE?

Common Daisy, the name does not do it justice because it is uncommonly magnificent to my eye (Loubigne, Western France).

Photography by the author.

THOU ARTE ILLUME

You`re a star yes you are

shining on so far

your're a gem, your're a jewel

so unique and so rare

with the world within your eyes

reflecting with your smile

that you give to everything

for you the flowers sing

All the beauty that you see

with every breath you take

so much more the world becomes

with a heart that beats as one

when the moon is shining bright

upon a starlit night

you bathe in silver rays

from the Goddess of the moon

thou arte illume

THE KEEPER OF LIFE

Oh flower what power do you hold may I know
your secrets in splendour, how is it you grow

Oh spider my spider, tell me how do you weave
as your webs become finer though flies never leave

Oh pasture green pasture, how is it your green
that seems to get lusher when more cows are seen

Oh feather light feather, tell me how do you fly
so weightless endeavours see more than may I

Oh keeper dear keeper, how is it you hold
such wonder to ponder, such food for the soul

Oh mother our mother, what things make you tick
with regular rhythm that never does slip

Oh teacher no preacher but wise that you are
you let us all learn by less and by far

I AM THEE

I AM divine, creative, feminine energy

spinning my spiral, maternal, eternal

i turn as the seasons, for they are my passing

ask of me all, I answer those asking

i am the source, the eye in the sky

i am your thoughts, your dreams by and by

serpent wisdom, serpent vision

mother, creator, destroyer, selector

huntress Selene, Isis your queen

guardian watcher, all nature, protector

i am all i am, you see

i am your wishes, i mote them so be

i am the spiral and the spiral is THEE

ALBION OF MY HEART

Albion of my heart
with each beat you call
Albion of my soul
we`ll meet again

Native i am of these mystical lands
Albion a dream that never ends

Your roots are mine together entwined
encoded in memory
in Albion's garden of my heart

From the time of the Picts, through ages not dark
Celtic to Roman, then Saxons they came
Danelaw of the Danes, all left their mark
Viking and Jute, within Albion`s heart

Though many a tribe rekindled the fire
and battles they came when tribal war reigned
many made home upon your sweet shores
in valleys so green
by ocean and river

raised there their corn
by Earth, Air, Fire and Water

Albion of my heart know thy thee so well
but never can we know of all that you`ve seen
so mote it be, the awen that flows mystically
in Albion`s secret alchemy

Beech trees, Avebury Stone Circle, Wiltshire, U.K.

Photgraphy by the author - 2010

OPEN YOUR HEART

If there ever was a wind that could blow so strong
to breeze into your mind like a long lost song
echoes of eternity that filter down to you
unlocking secret memories to give them back anew

If there ever was an ocean that could reach into your soul
to wash away your fears with the tides that roll
cleansing deep emotion now served it's time
returning with devotion all the things you find sublime

If there ever was a Sunrise that could bring you light within
to shine into your heart for a new day to begin
inspiring inner vision, see where you have flown
to reach a place inside where love is all you've known

MEMORY IN STONE

There is a memory within each stone
unique, to each their own
rushng down rivers and washed up on shores
each stone a reminder of what went before

There is a memory within each stone
that we feel with our hands and feel with our minds
and our minds are like the stone
yet who can see them grow?

Ever forming, evolving, elementary shining
actions of ice
water and weather that weathers the form
furnaced by fire, thrown into the air
riven into, broken in shards
rolled on the ground and waiting to be found
so close to us is stone

There is a memory within each stone
never rudimentary
but formed in complexity
a molecular symphony
set in the heart of stone

HEl HELD HERE

When we leave here you are no longer with us
you are what we see now, past this we cannot know
let not that be a barrier but a way between us
for look at how you are mirrored by minds
created upon wood and stone and blade
ring and pendant and buckle
carved in your name to honour this that is you
that is Hel

We see you, our thoughts manifested
our craft and our words given voice through time
the face of you as all we see you are
glimpses intuitive yet still you're not there
not waiting to embrace us with an icy cold stare
visage highlighted, half black and half white
personification of death yet life
as certain as the setting Sun

Dust falls down to settle old scores in the passing of mortal things
the passing and the crossing, that place that end
Hel stands at this side past that she's not there
past our reflection upon death in our minds
reminding us of all that we are, where resides a soul truly?
we hail you Hel, for you are so true
you count our days beyond our reckoning eyes
you see our frailty become more fragile with age
from newborn to our senior days

we ask not where you are
for you are always here, present in our lives
though never shall we meet again when we reach the other side
your not there

The die is cast before us, you rolled out the bones
seen within visions and marked with our tongues
recorders inscribed on parchment to witness the unseen
your face is the face of our mortal selves, the key to your court
that we enter alone

our days see much labour all told, our resting by hearth sees much fire
we placed you there past our reach or be scolded and scorned
we set your throne beyond embers and sparks
flying upon the winds of our times
so cold to our hearts
Hel in your realm so regally instated
not there when our fire is out

*Hel means "hidden" in Old Norse
23/03 2018

HEL FOR ALL

We each have our unique peception and as i am very eclectic with regards to pagan traditions and not being of any particular one but rather benefiting from the wisdom and insights that i can gleam from many, i can look at a goddess like Hel free from any dogma, i see her through my own eyes.

Given that i am aware of reincaranation and the existence of a soul i cannot see the goddess Hel as one that cares for the dead in the underworld because the dead are just physical shells whereas the soul/consciousness lives on. Hel to my mind is a representation of death itself and therefore equally she represents life, and i will touch on that later on. Hel serves as a reminder of death, a mnemonic (a system such as a pattern of letters, ideas, or associations which assists in remembering something).

Our need to come to terms with mortality is an intrinsic part of our human makeup, as mortality is an ever present and lurking factor whithin all our lives, it never leaves our side throughtout the span of our lives it stands silently watchhing, waiting, yet past death Hel is no longer. We came to hear of Hel through the writings of the Icelander Snorri Sturlusen (1179 – 23 September 1241) less that a thousand years ago, who, like myself, was a poet, he was also an historian and a politician. The (prose) Edda is a book of Icelandic sagas, no doubt based on a mixture of oral traditions passed down through families, stories used to inspire people within communities, stories to educate people and stories to explain our universe.and they are regarded by some with a certain amount of religiosity, though they are of course not religious texts, however they do contain magical elements so one can see them as magical and certainly enchanting, they speak of gods and goddesses and giants and creation myths in amazingly graphic detail. There is enchantment wihin the stories but the Nordic afterlife portrayed retains a very physical sense and that is realistic in some sense because all we can know here is what we see and experience here and as we cannot see and experience the beyond, at least not in our physical form, then attributing it with very physical aspects is an undestandable solution, especially useful for storytelling.

The Nordic people being extremely down to Earth and pragmatic had their pantheon of gods and goddesses that by tradition they acknowledged and there were also the wise ones who they respected and listened to but only when they needed to. Magical practices were not for everyday folk busy about their daily tasks, those that could divine and read the runes were, like the wise folk found everywhere, not common. It is wise to bare in mind that Snorri was a poet, a storyteller and the sagas he reinterpreted and added to, like they did with The Bible, were, unlike the bible, intended for the purpose of enjoyment and education and the perpetuation of the ethnic mythos of the Nordic people, to keep alive the custom of storytelling that serves as a cultural guidestone. However you see Hel let that be so and if you follow the sagas and see her as a carer of the dead in the underworld then all good and well.

Although i cannot see Hel as a goddess caring for the dead in the underworld i can however see her as representing the twin aspects of life and death (white and black) one side of her face is white for life and the other black for death, the hidden side. Hel means "hidden" in old Norse, because we cannot physically see beyond life to death. It really does not matter how you come to her in understanding as her presence wihin the sagas serves the purpose intended.
The goddess Hel bares no relationship to The cultural/christo-religious construct personification that has Hel as a wicked place of perpetual torment and servitude, and now spelt Hell, ruled over by a dominating yet male figure who holds his power over his minions residing in his underworld kingdom of brimestone and fire, where souls in torment enslaved in perpetual bondage exist in fear of the horned and tailed red devil bearing a trident, who can also influence the living by bending their minds to his will.

This oppressive, and dare i say impressive, construct certainly is one that has held so many in fear by the Christian church over the centuries, a grand deception courtesy of the religious authority of the Vatican. Those that remain in a state of fear are those that are able to be manipulated and is'nt it rather curious that the yarn that was spun pertaining to Hel(l) reflects the very intention and action of those that created it, to keep tormented souls in fear and thus servitude in perpetual bondadge to the will of the Christian church.

These days such a control device is not viable and with the advent of instant information new generations are discovering something of our ancestral past, a part of our heritage and so It is no wonder then that the Nordic underworld goddess is recognized now, in our times.

The christian concept has been imbedded within the minds of countless generations of people and even though you may not care for such a concept , it has played a big part in the pyscho/spiritual evolution of western religion and this affects the western mind set, consciouly or subconsciouly and mainly the latter, so it is not something that can easily be ignored as it has been a significant formulative factor within western rationale. In these enlightened days where one can now access information at the flick of the wrist, the tap of a key, the opportunity to discover that which our minds may desire holds an enticing possibility, a possibilty that cannot resist temptation. We can consider ,compare, evaluate and research and in so doing we are offered multiple choices and sometimes revelation. What was lost is being regained, despite the technological revolution and indeed aided by the technological revolution. The old ways hold firm, they call us to our roots and give back to us our power, our sovreignity.

Hel reminds us of our frailty but she also reminds us of our power, our innate power. the serpent energy that is within, that bares divine wisdom, that guides us, for it is the force of nature itself, the life force, the soul.
So, Hel not only represents death, that certain end of physical self, but also life, for equal to death is life, one exists because of the other, in balance. Because our bodies live our bodies die and because our bodies die we must live life to the full.

Within The (prose) Edda Hel is mostly only mentioned in passing. Snorri describes her appearance as being half-black, half-white, and with a perpetually grim and fierce expression on her face. Many scholars view Hel as more of a literary personification of the grave rather than a goddess who was actually worshiped or appeased in her own right but none of this really matters, it is what she means to us that is umportant. For me gods and goddesses remain as personifying figures, devices by which to relate to aspects of life and nature.

Poetic license is a form of magic when that license is given to magical minds and let us not forget that there is a light hearted air to all this. By making his characters speak to us in very human ways, ways that everyone can relate to, Snorri provided the bridge, the connection to experience his work on a very personal level but it should not be a dogmatic connection, that was not his intention. he wrote the sagas to be enjoyed.

MEMORY IN STONE

There is a memory within each stone
unique, to each their own
rushng down rivers and washed up on shores
each stone a reminder of what went before

There is a memory within each stone
that we feel with our hands and feel with our minds
and our minds are like the stone
yet who can see them grow?

Ever forming, evolving, elementary shining
actions of ice
water and weather that weathers the form
furnaced by fire, thrown into the air
riven into, broken in shards
rolled on the ground and waiting to be found
so close to us is stone

There is a memory within each stone
never rudimentary
but formed in complexity
a molecular symphony
set in the heart of stone

THE BAREFOOTED WYTCH (It Is So)

Through tangled woods where strangled by vine

trees squeeze to grow

feet on soft soil, dark rich and cool, a' wonering they must go

the barefooted wytch in nature so rich, wildness from tip to toe

so still it is there with myriad airs ,so surely it is so

there is no compare to a wood when you roam

where nature leads you home

From halcyon days to mid summer's haze, the bounty of it all
through autumnal rays and darkening ways
of winter's timely call
the stillness remains ever present refrain
as light plays through the trees
where shimmering leaves wait for a breeze
to become the ground again
The barefooted wytch is a wytch that knows
that which grows so wild
is the purest of heart and sacred thou arte
the wytch is nature's child
to be as one with nature's song where wytch's feet may go
is a blessing indeed with lessons to heed
so surely it is so

ABOUT THE AUTHOR

I was born in Guildford in the county of Surrey in England on the 20th February 1965, which makes me a snake according to the Chinese zodiac, which runs on a twelve year cycle. The snake can represent many things to many people but it is

universally known through the ages as a representation of the life force wihin and innate wisdom. Maybe the longheld association with snakes, wisdom and life force harks back to our primeval selves and our reptilian brain, encoded in our genetic memory.

In some North American native traditions my time of birth associates me with wolf/coyote. Many tribes are of the wolf/coyote clan, this makes perfect sense to me as personally i have a great afinity with these animals and my spirit name is RayneboWolf, this name was given to me intuitively by a psychic in 2007, though i have long known that i am of wolven kind.

I am an eclectic pagan and that suits my nature very well as i enjoy the diversity of human consciousness exploration and a myriad of spiriitual traditions forms a tapestry of insight, colour, wisdom, passion and mystique within my mind.

I am a child of the 1960's, we are called generation x, we where born into a world of revolution, idealism and ideas that seemed fantastic and this environment was our nurturing sustinance from infancy to child to teen to adulthood, it formulated our awareness, it was a unique juncture in history and it was a jumping point from passive acceptance into the turbulant waters of self exploration.
Alongside the rebellious nature of my youth came a sense of the divine that i could not define ,yet kept calling me. A magical moment at 15 within a stone circle, alone and afar on a moor, Stanton Moor, that place holds a magic of ancient charm and it changed me.

Later in my teens i used to spend spellbound, seemingly timeless charmed moments in a wonderful little old bookshop called Occultique in Northampton which specialized in new and second hand esoteric books, tarot cards, herbs, incense and magical regalia. The shop was established in 1973 and was very well known amongst pagans of all persuasions from all over the country and it was always very pleasant to meet people and chat quietly within that haven of peace and spiritual balance, a refuge in the town, that took me far from the maddening crowd, that i would always enjoy returning to over the years.

ABOUT MY FORNAMES

Salena is the Hindi derivation of the name of the Greek Moon goddess Selene and as such is a personification of Shakti, divine feminine creative power, the great divine mother. Shakti is also kundalini serpent energy that rises up through our chakras. Shakti is the cosmic agent of creation, change and liberation.

I was married in the United States of America in 2008 (now divorced) I have also lived in France for 3 years and 11 months (with 3 months away in the jungle in Costa Rica in Central America and 7 months in Ecuador in South America). I came back to the U.K in late 2013.

Brightest Blessings

Salena Shakti Radford

The author - June 2015

*** the cover photograph is an actual photograph of a face that i saw in an Ash tree by a healing well near Broughton, Northamptonshire, U.K - 2007.**

INTRODUCTION

Words can carry us to places within an instant, a whole world appears within our imagination without any conscious effort. A wordsmith crafts words upon the lathe of the psyche to fashion them and arrange them. From the initial spark of inspiration is borne a new realm of adventure within our mind's.

Presented within these pages you will find a selection of poems that focus upon our spiritual connection to all in nature, indeed we are nature. A poetic mind has many a muse but my muse of muses is the Earth herself.

*** the cover photograph is an actual photograph of a face i saw in an Ash tree by a healing well near Broughton, Northamptonshire, U.K - 2007.**

THE EARTH IS DREAMING

the Earth is dreaming to the Moon`s lullaby
the Earth is dreaming with a tearful eye
the Earth is dreaming to awaken visions
the Earth is dreaming and making decisions

The Earth is dreaming of different ways
the Earth is dreaming within all our days
the Earth is dreaming of things that are strange
the Earth is dreaming of all we arrange

The Earth is dreaming of plentiful grain
the Earth is dreaming to protect her name
the Earth is dreaming and seeing what grows
the Earth is dreaming accounting with crows

The Earth is dreaming and dreaming awake
the Earth is dreaming of mountains that shake
the Earth is dreaming of wasteful toil
the Earth is dreaming of replenished fertile soil

The Earth is dreaming though turns not to sleep
the Earth is dreaming but to us she speaks

Knap Hill Neolithic Causewayed Enclosure, Northeast of Alton Barnes, Wiltshire, U.K.

View from the parking area near the summit, as the Moon was rising through the Hawthorn tree. Just below the summit you can see the ditchres of the causewayed enclosure.

Photography by the author - 2007

THE LANGUAGE OF NATURE

What words are whispered amidst green leaves

high up on their branches catching light for the trees

what wisdom is spoken by the flower and the bee

what song is there sung in their sacred harmony

What is there spoken in the lay of the land
what words lie unbroken in what tongue to understand
what can be heard by the wild water's side
in voices so many over stones passing by

What message does a call from a bird bring swift
from the heart of nature and hard to be missed
what echo returns that calls to the soul
in the language of nature that speaks to us all.

Swallowhead Springs, the source of the River Kennet, near West Kennet Long Barrow and Silbury Hill, Wiltshire, U.K.

Sawllowhead Springs is an ancient sacred place of palpable energy.

Incidentally, the bridge where the river Kennet flows past Silbury Hill and under the A4 (old Roman road) is called Pan bridge. Pan is the Greek god of the wild, shepherds and flocks, mountainous wilds, rustic music and companion of the Nymphs, he has the hindquarters, legs and horns of a goat. Nymphs are divine spirits who animate nature and love to dance and sing and dwell within mountainous places, forests and by lakes and streams.

Photography by the author - 2007.

LISTEN TO THE EARTH

There was once a time that we may return again
in half forgotten fables that tell of the story when
many mighty stones were there across the sacred land
still they whisper to those that care that listen if they can

For so far that we`ve come we`ve lost our sight of Earth
so far away from the rites that held our place of birth
of the green man and the corn, the Goddess in the land
lets listen to the Earth again, so come now take my hand

I`ll lead you to the faerie fey for they reside at will
in a place not on this Earth but found within the hills
they too like the old ones see the passing years
that lead on to eternity, within their timeless spheres

What then shall befall us if we disconnect ourselves
from enchanted faerie glens and no more speak of elves?
all the magic that binds us to the very Earth around
for answers lie within herself, within her sacred ground

No matter how we perceive the truth shall always hold
from the wisdom of the old ones to the faerie kin extolled
if we foster compassion each within our hearts

we can hear the beat of Earth, the rhythm of the dance

unfolding for eternity in deep felt mirth, entranced

View from within a crop formation in a field of Barley of Silbury Hill, a Neolithic chalk and earth stepped spiral mound, Wiltshire, U.K.

Photography by the author - 2010

DRAGON OF THE EARTH

The dragon that lies within the land

known throughout time

and under the lines of the ley

as Earth energy that comes to rise

and spiral where it may

a potent force that gathers from the deep

to rise up through the earth

and once I believe harnessed

and set to work

where by the stones that mark it`s course

channel and focus this serpent like horse

though by agreement of mutual worth

measured by respect

for the dragon of the Earth

Were then, some of the white horses that we see

from Uffington Hill

to Wiltshire`s chalky Avalonian vales

once in the form of dragons with tails?

so named is such a mound

to be found close by to the giant white beast

who`s sheer size astounds

those who climb upon it`s back

Dragon Hill to be exact

close by to the ancient Ridgeway track

Did they tell of the tales that told

of the dragon lines

that wind. never straight but serpentine

of lore forgotten but still there to find?

And let us not forget Silbury Hill

having stood 5,000 years and more and standing still

as a testament to those times

when much was known of those dragon lines

this sacred spiral serpent mound

where the dragon rose and rises still

up to the sky bejewelled by stars

and back down again to the ground

Within the Earth the dragon dreams

sleeping sometimes but sure to awake

and sometimes even "seen" by those who can

if they possess the second sight

shimmering with electric light

as the dragon of the Earth

that winds through time

and comes to coil within our minds

Pine tree rings, Bucknell wood, near Towcester, Northamptonshire, U.K.

Photography by the author - 2007

THE WILDWOOD WITHIN

The morning mist now gently kissed

by the rising disc of the Sun

nostrils flare and sniff the fresh dampened air

listening now

the horned one surveys all that surrounds

before returning once again

to the woodland of his grounds

The owl calls from distant there within
as the blackbirds begin to sing
as the morning grows in glory
as the dawn slips away.
In the meadow by the brook
wild eyed hares leap and play

Enchanted by the wildwood`s call
touched by the very sanctity of life
called to a wild place within
to far forgotten days
when robin in the hood the spirit of the wood
and those that dwelled amidst the green
were more closely understood

As the pipes of Pan begin to play
the horned one some call Herne
and some call cernunnos
with great vigour leads the way
to the primeval part of us that knows
the very essence of nature
that shall ever flow
within our hearts
within our blood
and within our bones
to the balance of all things
that the Goddess has ordained

as sacred in her name

*** Robin is an old English word for spirit**
Hood is an old English word for wood.

The healing energy of trees can not only be felt but sometimes can also be seen.

A stand of trees, near the source of the The *Sèvre* Niortaise river near **Sepvret in Western France** in the Deux-*Sèvres* département, that flows into the Atlantic Ocean.

Photography by the author - 2010

A MOMENT OUT OF TIME

How the world seems kinder
when your thoughts all fall at ease
When feeling bright our hearts delight
upon such gentle breeze

Much there is that we can find
sublime and full of charm
this healing space that sees no haste
where there can be no harm

But for a moment out of time
serene and somewhere free
receiving this, a granted wish
no time brings more to please.

That which has now come to thee
resonates so fine
recalling dreams, forgotten themes
the world has left behind

Seize the day that brings thee bliss

how can we do much more

and all that is, that was that is

returns again for sure

Knowing that whatever comes

can`t steal this from our minds

upon the day we stole away

in a moment out of time

Barley softly sways and sings a sweeping song as it rustles with the breeze.

a field of barley next to Silbury Hill, Wiltshire, U.K.

photgraphy by the author - 2010

ENOSHA`S DREAM

As i lay in reverie
upon Wayland Smithy's mound
half awaking from a dream
on such a sacred ground
i heard a lady say to me
as clearly as the day
just two simple whispered words
that somehow seemed profound

"Enosha's dream" i heard her say
then no more then did she speak
but so refreshed was i that day
by my reverie
i rose up from that place
from my sanctuary of sleep
upon Wayland`s mound
where i was cradled deep

In this place of ancient rites

hallowed pagan shrine

did you here then preside

by an altar to divine?

or did you come to this place

that many still hold dear

an acolyte to worship

what the powers came to fear?

Long before the church did smite

with such a heavy hand

that breached into the pagan heart

and reached across the land

long before those wretched days

of outlawed pagan ways

our ancestors to the Earth

Goddess homage made

Wayland Smithy, near the Ridgeway Track, Oxfordshire, U.K.

Photography by the author - 2010

WITHIN HER HANDS

For one to hold within their hands

a precious gem so very rare

knowing it`s worth beyond all compare

would not they wish that it not drop

lie broken by lack of care?

The Earth is such a many faceted jewel

sharing and caring, though sometimes destroying

in all her greatness great and small

Now once we had an understanding

a way of more harmoniously existing

making careful use of each resource

but what began with simple needs

gathering, hunting, planting seeds

with the need to harvest fare

became the rape of land and air

The waters from her sacred springs

tainted some, by death machines

but like the river flowing on

we can become to see as one

She beckons us within her ways

calling clarion that we may

breathe as one upon this land

and see the precious gem in hand

for she holds us in her care

and with her then we need to share

not just take to make all

the fattest bellies remain full

as the more we take in our abstraction

fatal becomes this world`s attraction

and as all the children need to know

all things come but sometimes go

Walker's Hill (with Adam's Grave - burial mound on top) to the left of the photograph and Knap Hill to the right define the Goddess in the land lying down on her side with the top half of her body twisted to the sky. Knap Hill becomes her left thigh whilst adam's grave atop walker's hill becomes her right breast, as viewed from East Field, Alton Barnes, Wiltshire, U.K.

Photography by the author - 2010

WITHIN THE GREENWOOD GLADE

Come enter the greenwood
answer Bealtaine's call
leave aside past season's woes
for now no leaves do fall
if only for a spell they go
then cast your mind to play
for new loves with hearts aglow
are greening in the May

To bind their dreams as they entwine
within the glade unseen
with the joy of columbine
the ivy grows so keen
the scent of blooms pervades the air
come drink a hearty fill
for nature nurtures all with care
the glory of her will

In the grass so verdant green
lies the morning dew

the spider's web no more unseen

beaded now to view

reveals within it`s tapestry

the subtle flow of life

for weaved within the chemistry

more than meets the eye

*** Bealtaine: Gaelic May festival - pronounced B`yul-tin-ar**

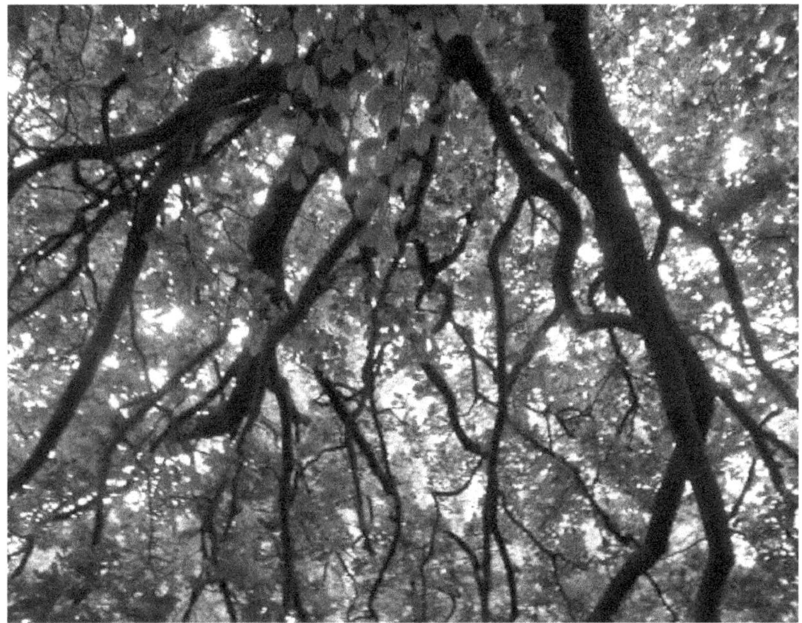

Beech Tree Canopy, Avebury Stone Circle, Wiltshire, U.K

Photography by the author - 2010

THE SISTERS OF WYRD

Like a sailor who sails the seven seas

seeking as they sail for their golden ship of dreams

set sail on some destiny

where fate and fortune change the wyrd web we see

All those things that we thought we had planned

oh for the lines that lie upon our hands

and the rainbow is only ever true

right where you stand and not some other's view

Like a moth too close to the flame

lured by something bright that may lead us blind

to where we wish we had never came

given wings to fly as the wyrd web unwinds

Such a thing the wyrd sisters weave

by our actions we may learn by all that we perceive

taking account of ourselves

with each silver strand into the web we delve

As we go we can change our path

for many strands may lead to the things that we may need

and all that we see is what we are

in all this universe in each and every star

Upon our travels that may take us far

sometimes the hurt that we feel leaves with us a scar

All this the wyrd sisters weave

all things that through many ways we come to perceive

As the wyrd sisters weave along your trail

consider the cup that you hold may not be full of jewels

but all that is revealed becomes our quested grail

A WYRD WORLD AND THE GODDESSES OF DESTINY

WYRD

Wyrd is the life we live and that which shall become. Wyrd is a web upon which we navigate our paths where each step creates a vibration that ripples out across all the strands of the wyrd web of life. Wyrd is life interconnecting, nothing exists entire of itself, it is cause and effect, balance and responsibility.

THE THREE NORNS

In Saxon mythology Wyrd carries the same meaning portrayed in Nordic mythology by The Three Norns (there is a thin line between Nordic and Saxon mythology and ancient art) The Three Norns are the Goddesses of destiny and they are called Urd "What Once Was" Verdandi "What Is Coming into Being" and Skuld "What Shall Be". The Wyrd Sisters in Shakespear's play A Midsummer's Night Dream were based upon the three norns.

Glastonbury Tor and St Michael's Tower, all that remains of the 14th century church that once stood atop the tor.

It is also known as the Isle of Avalon. Two thousand years ago the sea washed up to the foot of the Tor, so it would have been an island. Avalon was also called the isle of glass and it would have appeared that it was on glass when surrounded by water. Ancient myth tells of Avalon as being the meeting place of the dead, a liminal realm where the sea meets the land and there is a legend that king Arthur was buried upon the Isle of Avalon. Welsh tradition sees the Tor as the home of Gywn Ap Nudd, lord of the underworld, a place where fairies live.

Around the Tor and winding up to the top is a system of terraces that some suggest are man made, they are weathered but still well definded so if you fancy another way to the summit then walking the terraces is an interesting option.

Legend has it that Joseph of Arimathea (jesus's uncle) buried the grail cup from jesus's last supper at the foot of the Tor.

At the base of the Tor is Chalice well, the water has a reddish tinge to it due to it's iron rich content.

Photography by the author - 2010

ALL SOULS KNOW WELL OF SOULS

The tangled path of time obscure
yet with wit we can traverse
all the woes that we endure
to reach the well with mighty thirst

Shining each in radiant light
unfettered our wings, unfurled ascend
to the well of souls we take our flight
where ancient hearts may meet again

The source of us, become immersed
drink deeply of the waters there
where gathered souls have come to share
where wisdom sings within the air

Back to the Earth we may choose to go
to see again through worldly eyes
yet that choice is hard to tell

upon returning from the well

ANOTHER SPIRIT LEVEL:

THE SPIRIT OF H20

(a reflection upon and within water)

What a clear thought can achieve
by the solution of water
that flows with ease
is anything that we please
homoeopathically distilling
whatever is given
the wonder of water
is a blessing indeed

Water it seems has many solutions
by whatever it holds
within it`s dimension
the water that we bless
is water at it`s best
and wherever in this world
you may be

water reaches thee
flowing into the streams
into the rivers
and into the sea
can we then see a world in love
unconditional, joyful and free?

So let`s drink a toast
to the mighty water spirit
molecular, dynamic
crystalline and clear
raising consciousness on our planet
by the magic of water
may our visions appear

Any intention exerted
whether large or small
can create a change
from a giant wave tsunami
to a wonderful waterfall

If you speak to water
it reacts within its system
corresponding to your intent
then taking shape to implement

within its structure, cellular change

and once within the system

flows where water flows

into the streams into the rivers

into the oceans of the world

carrying the words that you gave it

that shape its inner form

the water then to be drunk

imbued by one and all

then what was given

as we are water based

becomes the way that we feel

and the way that we relate

So lets give love to water

by the power of our words

and stop and think!

each time we drink

about how we wish to be

maybe this world we can refresh

by water's wonderful memory?

FLUTTER BY WINGS

With wings that flutter myriad
in utter splendid colour
but butter not are they
as they grace the garden
that attracts them to its elegant array
of Lepidoptera enticing flora
and once discovered
shall return each day
within their short span of life
or so it seems to us
who watch them flutter by
though it is fair to say
that they have two lives within one
and somewhere in the middle
get reformed and then reborn
from the caterpillar within the cocoon
the chrysalis that someday soon
shall yield the insect from within
completely changed from it`s former self
now adorned with splendid wings
to greet the day anen

THE CELTIC FLUTTER BY SOUL

Going back to times of yore
long, long before these days
where in the meadows
the flutter bys flexed their wings
and without the reflex of pins
alighted upon the wild flowers
free and without a care
so splendid as they are
they inspired the Celtic bards
to consider yet again who we really are
our own span of life and beyond to stars
this they did and they came to see
that the flutter-by was a soul
that had flown to the summer land
and now returned with wings so grand
and so what they knew too to be a flutter-by
and then so aptly termed
were the ancestors and the ones they loved
here again from the sweet fields above
and not something to be stuck with pins
but respected and cared for
these flutter-by wings
as those that return again and are reborn
not just in metaphor but also in form

manifested anew to greet a new dawn

Swallowtail butterfly, Loubigne, western France.

Photography by the author - 2010

BEHOLD THE BEE

Behold the humble honey bee

as it stumbles into flowers

pollinating as it goes

buzzing and brimming

with life giving powers

gathering sweet nectar

to honey your mead

and wax for the candles

that at night we may need

The humble honey bee

who shares it`s industry freely

to sweeten your bread

who by it`s labour may nurse a cold

with this food of the Gods

from days of old

known for it`s powers

to preserve and protect

for vitality and much more yet!

So set your thoughts to such a thing as a bee

as to be a bee that daily dives

from flower to flower

and back again to the hive

is to be free and to be free is to be alive

So blessed be the humble honey bee!

but where would we be if it was gone?

this one that is solar driven in it`s song

through all the days that seem so long

in sweet summers alchemy

where would we be?

Some things you see cannot be replaced

save for maybe our own human race

as we alone cannot go on

depending as we do upon

such things as the one who is solar driven in it`s song

through all the days that seem so long

in sweet summer's alchemy

So then it seems to be

that we cannot be without the BEE

Bumble Bee taking nectar from Lavender, Lounigne, Western France.

Photography by the author - 2010

ONE in LOVE

Each distant star carries with it a memory of our soul

our hearts are synchronised with the music of the spheres

our bodies are crystallised components of the Gods

Contained within each of us is the eternal chord

struck once at the very emergence of our universe

it holds our form, that which we choose to be, that which we dream we are
is not all life therefore magic, a shimmering facet of our desires?

Climbing the inner temple of our bodies
we reach the centre from which we observe all things
we open ourselves to realities that know no bounds or separation
only unity in divinity, that which we are

Casting aside the mask of illusion we see with eyes of awareness
perceiving our nature as a force of great power
free flowing thoughts that carry the whisper of bliss
bring joy to our lips as we acknowledge this
for our true strength lies within a smile that generates love and kindness

Compassion is the seed that flowers into love
that brings us back to us and links us into a hive of harmony
our consciousness unified
Is it not better to be ONE in LOVE?

Common Daisy, the name does not do it justice because it is uncommonly magnificent to my eye (Loubigne, Western France).

Photography by the author.

THOU ARTE ILLUME

You`re a star yes you are

shining on so far

your're a gem, your're a jewel

so unique and so rare

with the world within your eyes

reflecting with your smile

that you give to everything

for you the flowers sing

All the beauty that you see

with every breath you take

so much more the world becomes

with a heart that beats as one

when the moon is shining bright

upon a starlit night

you bathe in silver rays

from the Goddess of the moon

thou arte illume

THE KEEPER OF LIFE

Oh flower what power do you hold may I know
your secrets in splendour, how is it you grow

Oh spider my spider, tell me how do you weave
as your webs become finer though flies never leave

Oh pasture green pasture, how is it your green
that seems to get lusher when more cows are seen

Oh feather light feather, tell me how do you fly
so weightless endeavours see more than may I

Oh keeper dear keeper, how is it you hold
such wonder to ponder, such food for the soul

Oh mother our mother, what things make you tick
with regular rhythm that never does slip

Oh teacher no preacher but wise that you are
you let us all learn by less and by far

I AM THEE

I AM divine, creative, feminine energy

spinning my spiral, maternal, eternal

i turn as the seasons, for they are my passing

ask of me all, I answer those asking

i am the source, the eye in the sky

i am your thoughts, your dreams by and by

serpent wisdom, serpent vision

mother, creator, destroyer, selector

huntress Selene, Isis your queen

guardian watcher, all nature, protector

i am all i am, you see

i am your wishes, i mote them so be

i am the spiral and the spiral is THEE

ALBION OF MY HEART

Albion of my heart
with each beat you call
Albion of my soul
we`ll meet again

Native i am of these mystical lands
Albion a dream that never ends

Your roots are mine together entwined
encoded in memory
in Albion's garden of my heart

From the time of the Picts, through ages not dark
Celtic to Roman, then Saxons they came
Danelaw of the Danes, all left their mark
Viking and Jute, within Albion`s heart

Though many a tribe rekindled the fire
and battles they came when tribal war reigned
many made home upon your sweet shores
in valleys so green
by ocean and river

raised there their corn
by Earth, Air, Fire and Water

Albion of my heart know thy thee so well
but never can we know of all that you`ve seen
so mote it be, the awen that flows mystically
in Albion`s secret alchemy

Beech trees, Avebury Stone Circle, Wiltshire, U.K.

Photgraphy by the author - 2010

OPEN YOUR HEART

If there ever was a wind that could blow so strong
to breeze into your mind like a long lost song
echoes of eternity that filter down to you
unlocking secret memories to give them back anew

If there ever was an ocean that could reach into your soul
to wash away your fears with the tides that roll
cleansing deep emotion now served it's time
returning with devotion all the things you find sublime

If there ever was a Sunrise that could bring you light within
to shine into your heart for a new day to begin
inspiring inner vision, see where you have flown
to reach a place inside where love is all you've known

MEMORY IN STONE

There is a memory within each stone
unique, to each their own
rushng down rivers and washed up on shores
each stone a reminder of what went before

There is a memory within each stone
that we feel with our hands and feel with our minds
and our minds are like the stone
yet who can see them grow?

Ever forming, evolving, elementary shining
actions of ice
water and weather that weathers the form
furnaced by fire, thrown into the air
riven into, broken in shards
rolled on the ground and waiting to be found
so close to us is stone

There is a memory within each stone
never rudimentary
but formed in complexity
a molecular symphony
set in the heart of stone

HEl HELD HERE

When we leave here you are no longer with us
you are what we see now, past this we cannot know
let not that be a barrier but a way between us
for look at how you are mirrored by minds
created upon wood and stone and blade
ring and pendant and buckle
carved in your name to honour this that is you
that is Hel

We see you, our thoughts manifested
our craft and our words given voice through time
the face of you as all we see you are
glimpses intuitive yet still you're not there
not waiting to embrace us with an icy cold stare
visage highlighted, half black and half white
personification of death yet life
as certain as the setting Sun

Dust falls down to settle old scores in the passing of mortal things
the passing and the crossing, that place that end
Hel stands at this side past that she's not there
past our reflection upon death in our minds
reminding us of all that we are, where resides a soul truly?
we hail you Hel, for you are so true
you count our days beyond our reckoning eyes
you see our frailty become more fragile with age
from newborn to our senior days

we ask not where you are
for you are always here, present in our lives
though never shall we meet again when we reach the other side
your not there

The die is cast before us, you rolled out the bones
seen within visions and marked with our tongues
recorders inscribed on parchment to witness the unseen
your face is the face of our mortal selves, the key to your court
that we enter alone

our days see much labour all told, our resting by hearth sees much fire
we placed you there past our reach or be scolded and scorned
we set your throne beyond embers and sparks
flying upon the winds of our times
so cold to our hearts
Hel in your realm so regally instated
not there when our fire is out

*Hel means "hidden" in Old Norse
23/03 2018

HEL FOR ALL

We each have our unique peception and as i am very eclectic with regards to pagan traditions and not being of any particular one but rather benefiting from the wisdom and insights that i can gleam from many, i can look at a goddess like Hel free from any dogma, i see her through my own eyes.

Given that i am aware of reincaranation and the existence of a soul i cannot see the goddess Hel as one that cares for the dead in the underworld because the dead are just physical shells whereas the soul/consciousness lives on. Hel to my mind is a representation of death itself and therefore equally she represents life, and i will touch on that later on. Hel serves as a reminder of death, a mnemonic (a system such as a pattern of letters, ideas, or associations which assists in remembering something).

Our need to come to terms with mortality is an intrinsic part of our human makeup, as mortality is an ever present and lurking factor whithin all our lives, it never leaves our side throughtout the span of our lives it stands silently watchhing, waiting, yet past death Hel is no longer. We came to hear of Hel through the writings of the Icelander Snorri Sturlusen (1179 – 23 September 1241) less that a thousand years ago, who, like myself, was a poet, he was also an historian and a politician. The (prose) Edda is a book of Icelandic sagas, no doubt based on a mixture of oral traditions passed down through families, stories used to inspire people within communities, stories to educate people and stories to explain our universe.and they are regarded by some with a certain amount of religiosity, though they are of course not religious texts, however they do contain magical elements so one can see them as magical and certainly enchanting, they speak of gods and goddesses and giants and creation myths in amazingly graphic detail. There is enchantment wihin the stories but the Nordic afterlife portrayed retains a very physical sense and that is realistic in some sense because all we can know here is what we see and experience here and as we cannot see and experience the beyond, at least not in our physical form, then attributing it with very physical aspects is an undestandable solution, especially useful for storytelling.

The Nordic people being extremely down to Earth and pragmatic had their pantheon of gods and goddesses that by tradition they acknowledged and there were also the wise ones who they respected and listened to but only when they needed to. Magical practices were not for everyday folk busy about their daily tasks, those that could divine and read the runes were, like the wise folk found everywhere, not common. It is wise to bare in mind that Snorri was a poet, a storyteller and the sagas he reinterpreted and added to, like they did with The Bible, were, unlike the bible, intended for the purpose of enjoyment and education and the perpetuation of the ethnic mythos of the Nordic people, to keep alive the custom of storytelling that serves as a cultural guidestone. However you see Hel let that be so and if you follow the sagas and see her as a carer of the dead in the underworld then all good and well.

Although i cannot see Hel as a goddess caring for the dead in the underworld i can however see her as representing the twin aspects of life and death (white and black) one side of her face is white for life and the other black for death, the hidden side. Hel means "hidden" in old Norse, because we cannot physically see beyond life to death. It really does not matter how you come to her in understanding as her presence wihin the sagas serves the purpose intended.
The goddess Hel bares no relationship to The cultural/christo-religious construct personification that has Hel as a wicked place of perpetual torment and servitude, and now spelt Hell, ruled over by a dominating yet male figure who holds his power over his minions residing in his underworld kingdom of brimestone and fire, where souls in torment enslaved in perpetual bondage exist in fear of the horned and tailed red devil bearing a trident, who can also influence the living by bending their minds to his will.

This oppressive, and dare i say impressive, construct certainly is one that has held so many in fear by the Christian church over the centuries, a grand deception courtesy of the religious authority of the Vatican. Those that remain in a state of fear are those that are able to be manipulated and is'nt it rather curious that the yarn that was spun pertaining to Hel(l) reflects the very intention and action of those that created it, to keep tormented souls in fear and thus servitude in perpetual bondadge to the will of the Christian church.

These days such a control device is not viable and with the advent of instant information new generations are discovering something of our ancestral past, a part of our heritage and so It is no wonder then that the Nordic underworld goddess is recognized now, in our times.

The christian concept has been imbedded within the minds of countless generations of people and even though you may not care for such a concept , it has played a big part in the pyscho/spiritual evolution of western religion and this affects the western mind set, consciouls y or subconsciouly and mainly the latter, so it is not something that can easily be ignored as it has been a significant formulative factor within western rationale. In these enlightened days where one can now access information at the flick of the wrist, the tap of a key, the opportunity to discover that which our minds may desire holds an enticing possibility, a possibilty that cannot resist temptation. We can consider ,compare, evaluate and research and in so doing we are offered multiple choices and sometimes revelation. What was lost is being regained, despite the technological revolution and indeed aided by the technological revolution. The old ways hold firm, they call us to our roots and give back to us our power, our sovreignity.

Hel reminds us of our frailty but she also reminds us of our power, our innate power. the serpent energy that is within, that bares divine wisdom, that guides us, for it is the force of nature itself, the life force, the soul.
So, Hel not only represents death, that certain end of physical self, but also life, for equal to death is life, one exists because of the other, in balance. Because our bodies live our bodies die and because our bodies die we must live life to the full.

Within The (prose) Edda Hel is mostly only mentioned in passing. Snorri describes her appearance as being half-black, half-white, and with a perpetually grim and fierce expression on her face. Many scholars view Hel as more of a literary personification of the grave rather than a goddess who was actually worshiped or appeased in her own right but none of this really matters, it is what she means to us that is umportant. For me gods and goddesses remain as personifying figures, devices by which to relate to aspects of life and nature.

Poetic license is a form of magic when that license is given to magical minds and let us not forget that there is a light hearted air to all this. By making his characters speak to us in very human ways, ways that everyone can relate to, Snorri provided the bridge, the connection to experience his work on a very personal level but it should not be a dogmatic connection, that was not his intention. he wrote the sagas to be enjoyed.

MEMORY IN STONE

There is a memory within each stone
unique, to each their own
rushng down rivers and washed up on shores
each stone a reminder of what went before

There is a memory within each stone
that we feel with our hands and feel with our minds
and our minds are like the stone
yet who can see them grow?

Ever forming, evolving, elementary shining
actions of ice
water and weather that weathers the form
furnaced by fire, thrown into the air
riven into, broken in shards
rolled on the ground and waiting to be found
so close to us is stone

There is a memory within each stone
never rudimentary
but formed in complexity
a molecular symphony
set in the heart of stone

THE BAREFOOTED WYTCH (It Is So)

Through tangled woods where strangled by vine

trees squeeze to grow

feet on soft soil, dark rich and cool, a' wonering they must go

the barefooted wytch in nature so rich, wildness from tip to toe

so still it is there with myriad airs ,so surely it is so

there is no compare to a wood when you roam

where nature leads you home

From halcyon days to mid summer's haze, the bounty of it all
through autumnal rays and darkening ways
of winter's timely call
the stillness remains ever present refrain
as light plays through the trees
where shimmering leaves wait for a breeze
to become the ground again
The barefooted wytch is a wytch that knows
that which grows so wild
is the purest of heart and sacred thou arte
the wytch is nature's child
to be as one with nature's song where wytch's feet may go
is a blessing indeed with lessons to heed
so surely it is so

ABOUT THE AUTHOR

I was born in Guildford in the county of Surrey in England on the 20th February 1965, which makes me a snake according to the Chinese zodiac, which runs on a twelve year cycle. The snake can represent many things to many people but it is

universally known through the ages as a representation of the life force wihin and innate wisdom. Maybe the longheld association with snakes, wisdom and life force harks back to our primeval selves and our reptilian brain, encoded in our genetic memory.

In some North American native traditions my time of birth associates me with wolf/coyote. Many tribes are of the wolf/coyote clan, this makes perfect sense to me as personally i have a great afinity with these animals and my spirit name is RayneboWolf, this namc was given to me intuitively by a psychic in 2007, though i have long known that i am of wolven kind.

I am an eclectic pagan and that suits my nature very well as i enjoy the diversity of human consciousness exploration and a myriad of spiriitual traditions forms a tapestry of insight, colour, wisdom, passion and mystique within my mind.

I am a child of the 1960's, we are called generation x, we where born into a world of revolution, idealism and ideas that seemed fantastic and this environment was our nurturing sustinance from infancy to child to teen to adulthood, it formulated our awareness, it was a unique juncture in history and it was a jumping point from passive acceptance into the turbulant waters of self exploration.
Alongside the rebellious nature of my youth came a sense of the divine that i could not define ,yet kept calling me. A magical moment at 15 within a stone circle, alone and afar on a moor, Stanton Moor, that place holds a magic of ancient charm and it changed me.

Later in my teens i used to spend spellbound, seemingly timeless charmed moments in a wonderful little old bookshop called Occultique in Northampton which specialized in new and second hand esoteric books, tarot cards, herbs, incense and magical regalia. The shop was established in 1973 and was very well known amongst pagans of all persuasions from all over the country and it was always very pleasant to meet people and chat quietly within that haven of peace and spiritual balance, a refuge in the town, that took me far from the maddening crowd, that i would always enjoy returning to over the years.

ABOUT MY FORNAMES

Salena is the Hindi derivation of the name of the Greek Moon goddess Selene and as such is a personification of Shakti, divine feminine creative power, the great divine mother. Shakti is also kundalini serpent energy that rises up through our chakras. Shakti is the cosmic agent of creation, change and liberation.

I was married in the United States of America in 2008 (now divorced) I have also lived in France for 3 years and 11 months (with 3 months away in the jungle in Costa Rica in Central America and 7 months in Ecuador in South America). I came back to the U.K in late 2013.

Brightest Blessings

Salena Shakti Radford

The author - June 2015

*** the cover photograph is an actual photograph of a face that i saw in an Ash tree by a healing well near Broughton, Northamptonshire, U.K - 2007.**

www.ingramcontent.com/pod-product-compliance
Ingram Content Group UK Ltd.
Pitfield, Milton Keynes, MK11 3LW, UK
UKHW021528300726
14060UKWH00011B/32

9 780244 385224